Mom's
Handy Book of
BACKYARD
GAMES

Mom's
Handy Book of
BACKYARD
GAMES
by Pete Cava

Wish Publishing
Terre Haute, Indiana
www.wishpublishing.com

LCCN: 00-102418

Book edited by Holly Kondras
Proofread by Heather Lowhorn
Diagrams by Debbie Oldenburg
Cover designed by Phil Velikan

Printed in the United States of America
10 9 8 7 6 5 4 3 2 1

Published in the United States by
Wish Publishing
P.O. Box 10337
Terre Haute, IN 47801, USA
www.wishpublishing.com

Distributed in the United States by
Cardinal Publishers Group
Indianapolis, Indiana 46240

Wish Publishing would like to thank the children and parents who participated in the photography for this book: Amara Erickson, Jill Erickson, Jimmy Newton, Jessica Newton, Marquita Newton, Dorothy Pruitt, Logan Pruitt, Loren Pruitt, Jaylen Scott, Jansen Scott, Shelby Scott, Robbie Lynch, Jade Lynch, Jennifer Lynch and Lea Meck.

CONTENTS

PART II Ball Games   21

PART III Group Action Games   41

PART IV Hopping, Jumping and All Sorts of Games   69

PART V Word and Mind Games   87

Bibliography & Indexes 99

INTRODUCTION

One day, during a summer vacation at the New Jersey Shore, I witnessed an amazing development. A large group, consisting of several grown-ups and enough children to choke a van, arrived and claimed its section of beach. While the kids helped the grown-ups lay down blankets and set up beach umbrellas, one of the adult males began digging an elaborate sand castle with an army entrenching tool. Fascinated, I watched him dig — first a moat, then a spiraling mountain fortress with a winding highway that went all the way to the top. After completing this garrison, the man dumped out on the sand a box-load of soldiers and military ordnance that would have made General Patton green with envy. He then turned to the kids and said: "Have fun." Then he tossed his hat, t-shirt and sunglasses onto a blanket and took off for the surf while the kids began what turned out to be an all-day round of play on his marvelous mountain of sand.

When it came to child's play, that man had the right idea. Too often, adults stifle their children's natural creativity with supervised and well-defined (and well-intentioned) activities. Like that unknown Jersey Shore sand sculptor, this book aims to provide children with the groundwork for fun: activities with minimal adult supervision, and ground rules that the kids can bend and shape at will into their own form of entertainment.

The activities outlined on these pages range from ancient to very modern. Some games and rhymes were handed down by my grandparents to my mother and father, and from my wife and I to our own children. Others were spawned in the 1990s, when our kids and their playmates blasted off into that magic world of backyard play and were left to their own wonderful devices.

To kids everywhere — from Ralph, Janis, Carol, Regina, Albert, Raymond, Donald, Dougie, Andrew, Louie and the rest of my gang from so long ago; to Andy, Nancy, Kent, Brock, Jill, Jenny and the others who currently fan the flame of fun and play — this book is dedicated.

PART 1:

TAG, CHASE AND CATCH GAMES

1 Tag

Best for Ages: 5 and up

Number of Players Required: 3 or more

Equipment Needed: None

How to Play: One player is designated as "It," and one area — a tree, a section of fence, a porch, etc. — is selected as "base." As long as a player has physical contact with the base, It can't tag him. Once a player leaves base, however, It can give chase. Any player It touches away from base then becomes It. To lose the designation, It must tag another player. It's customary to say, "Tag, you're It!" when successfully tagging another player.

Playing tips:

★ To move the players off the base at the start of the game, It can count to a hundred by fives, and then chant: "Apples, peaches, pumpkin pie, anybody round my base is It!'"

★ After It tags a player, he can avoid being immediately tagged back by that player by saying: "You're It, no returns!" This exempts a player from being tagged again until after he returns to base, allowing him to catch his breath after chasing the players around the yard.

★ Instead of designating an area as "base," players can designate a material — wood, metal, concrete — as base. As long as players are in contact with that material, they can't be tagged by It.

2 Beckons Wanted

Best for Ages: 7 and up
Number of Players Required: 3 or more
Equipment Needed: None
How to Play: This is a nighttime version of Hide and Seek, with a fun variation. One player becomes It, and one area is designated as home base. While It closes his eyes and counts to 20, the rest run and hide. When It finishes counting, he says: "Ready or not, here I come, beckons wanted!" At this command, the players must make a nighttime sound like a hooting owl, a mosquito's buzz...even a lion's roar, to add to the spookiness of a game played in the gloaming. It can call "Beckons Wanted" at any time, and each time the players must answer with a sound. While It searches for the players, anyone who gets back to home base without being tagged is safe. The first player tagged becomes It, and the game starts over.

3 Blindfold Tag

Best for Ages: 7 and up
Number of Players Required: 3 or more
Equipment Needed: Blindfold
How to Play: This is a Tag variation. Designate a smaller area for the playing area and blindfold It. When It calls the name of any player, that player has to answer: "Here I am!" The real fun in this variation comes when the players try to get as close to It as possible without getting caught.

4 Capture the Flag

Best for Ages: 7 and up

Number of Players Required: 2 teams of 3 or more

Equipment Needed: 2 flags

How to Play: Depending on the terrain, Capture the Flag can range over several backyards. As many as four or more backyards make for a great playing field for any number of players. Players are divided into sides, and each team has an object that serves as a flag — a shirt, jacket or even a rag will do.

The playing field is divided into two equal halves, one for each side. Each side hides its flag in its own territory. After the flags are concealed, each side signals the other that they're ready to begin. Players must then try to discover the opposing team's flag and bring it back to their own side without being tagged. A player who enters enemy territory can be tagged by members of the opposing team. When tagged, a player has to go to a "Prison" area and can only be released when tagged by a member of her own team.

On their own territory, players can't be tagged by members from the opposite team. When a player discovers the opposing team's flag, she tries to get it back to her own territory without being tagged. The game ends when a team captures their opponents' flag.

5 Chain Tag

Best for Ages: 5 and up
Number of Players Required: 3 or more
Equipment Needed: None
How to Play: In this version, when It tags one of the players they join hands. They continue playing, and each player tagged joins the chain. The game continues until all players are part of the chain. The last player tagged is It for the next round.

6 Chinese Tag

Best for Ages: 5 and up
Number of Players Required: 5 to 10
Equipment Needed: None
How to Play: Nobody's sure about how this game got its name, but chances are it really didn't originate in China! Whenever It tags someone, that player becomes It — and also has to place a hand over the part of the body that was tagged. For instance, if a player is tagged on the arm, the player becomes It and can chase after other players, but only as long as he's got a hand on the part of his arm that was tagged. He can't use that hand to tag another player.

Playing tip:

★ Try to avoid being tagged on the leg or foot! Even Carl Lewis would have trouble trying to catch someone while holding on to his calf or his heel.

7 Detective's Trail

Best for Ages: 7 and up

Number of Players Required: 2

Equipment Needed: 2 paper bags and either bright-colored stones, bright strips of cloth or even bright-colored pieces of paper.

How to Play:

This game is a lot more fun in backyards with plenty of trees, bushes, fences, walls and even steps. The players mark off an area as home base, or "Robber's Den," and decide which player will be the Robber and which player will be the Detective. When the Robber leaves, the Detective remains at home base, hiding his eyes and counting to a hundred. The Robber carries a paper bag filled with the stones, cloth or paper, and begins marking a trail that the Detective must follow. While the Robber tries to get back to his den, the Detective must follow the trail, picking up each stone, paper or piece of cloth and placing it in his bag. The Robber doesn't hide, but tries to stay far ahead of the Detective, who has to stick to the trail and pick up every "clue" — even if the Robber starts to run for it. If the Robber starts running, he has to leave a trail for the detective to follow. The Detective can run after the Robber, as long as the Detective picks up all the "clues." If the Detective catches the Robber before he can get back to the Robber's Den, the players change sides.

Playing tip:

★   The Robber should always try to make the trail as complicated as possible by going in circles around the trees, going up and down the steps, under bushes, etc.

8 Duck, Duck, Goose

Best for Ages: 7 and up

Number of Players Required: 12 or more

Equipment Needed: None

How to Play: To start the game, one player is chosen as It. The remaining players sit cross-legged in a circle, facing inward. Walking clockwise around the players, It touches each one, saying "Duck." When It touches a player and says "Goose," he begins to run. So does the player he touched, but counterclockwise. Both try to get to the empty spot in the circle. If It gets there first, then the player becomes It. If not, It has to go again.

Variations:

Instead of running counterclockwise, the player touched by It runs after him. If the player tags It before It gets to the empty spot in the circle, then It must go again. There's another version (sometimes called "Drop the Handkerchief") that keeps all players on their toes. Instead of sitting, the players stand in a circle, singing: *A tisket, a tasket, A green and yellow basket. I wrote a letter to my love, And on the way I dropped it. A little doggy picked it up, And put it in his pocket.*

While the players sing, It jogs clockwise around the circle, carrying a handkerchief. As he passes each player, It says: "I won't bite you . . . I won't bite you . . . I won't bite you." When It passes a player who looks like she's not paying attention, It drops the handkerchief, saying: "But I will bite you!" It and the player race in opposite directions for the empty spot in the circle.

9 Flashlight Tag

Best for Ages: 7 and up

Number of Players Required: 3 or more

Equipment Needed: Flashlight

How to Play: This is a nighttime variation of Tag. It requires set boundaries. After It and the base area are chosen, the players scatter while It closes his eyes and counts to a hundred by fives. The players hide from It, and try to get to base while he comes after them. If It shines the flashlight on a player, that player becomes It.

10 Fox and Geese

Best for Ages: 5 and up

Number of Players Required: 3 to 6

Equipment Needed: Snow

How to Play: Here's a game for a snow-covered backyard. The players make a large circle with spokes in the snow. The center of the wheel is home base. One player is chosen as the fox. The rest of the players are the geese, and the fox tries to catch them. All players, fox and geese alike, cannot leave the paths. When the fox catches a goose, the players change places and the game continues.

11 Freeze Tag

Best for Ages: 7 and up
Number of Players Required: 3 or more
Equipment Needed: None
How to Play: Here's another Tag spin-off in which players tagged by It immediately stop moving. Those players must remain immobile until "unfrozen" — that is, tagged by another player and set free. This version works best with a time limit.

12 Gray Ghost

Best for Ages: 7 and up
Number of Players Required: 3 or more
Equipment Needed: None
How to Play: This Tag variant can be played from dusk to dark. One player is chosen as the Gray Ghost. The remaining players gather in an area designated as base — near a tree, porch, fence, etc. — and count to a hundred while the Gray Ghost hides. When the count reaches one hundred, all players must run around the house in the same direction, trying to return to base without getting caught by the Gray Ghost. If the Gray Ghost tags a player, that person becomes the Gray Ghost for the next round. If the Gray Ghost fails to tag anyone before the players reach base, he remains the Gray Ghost for another round.

13 Hide and Seek

Best for Ages: 7 and up
Number of Players Required: 6 or more
Equipment Needed: None
How to Play: A player is chosen as It. An area (tree, porch, section of fence, etc.) is chosen as base. Standing near base, It hides his eyes and counts to a hundred by fives while the other players scatter. When he sees a player, It calls the player's name and his location: "Andy by the woodpile!" That player and It run toward the goal. Whoever gets there last is It.

Variation:

Sometimes this game is called "I Spy," and when It sees a player he says: "I spy Andy by the woodpile," or "I spy Kent by the pine tree."

14 How Deep is the Water?

Best for Ages: 5 and up

Number of Players Required: 2 or more

Equipment Needed: None

How to Play: This game comes from Central Europe, and can be played by any number, 5 or older. Players draw two lines on the ground, about 15 feet apart. One player is chosen as the Fisherman and stands in the middle. The rest, who are the fish, stand behind one of the lines, which are "riverbanks." The Fish ask, "Fisherman, Fisherman, how deep is the river?" The Fisherman replies with a number. "Fisherman, Fisherman," ask the Fish, "how can we cross?" The Fisherman comes up with an appropriate answer. If the water is low, they can fly (the players do this by flapping their arms). If it's deep, they can swim (making swimming motions as they go across). At the command, the Fish try to get across to the other riverbank. Any player who is tagged joins the Fisherman as he tries to catch the Fish. The last uncaught Fish gets to be the Fisherman for the next round.

15 Kick the Can

Best for Ages: 7 and up

Number of Players Required: 4 to 10

Equipment Needed: An empty can

How to Play: In a "Twilight Zone" episode, a group of elderly people try to regain their youth by playing Kick the Can, a game that seems like it's been around forever.

The best setting for Kick the Can is an area with plenty of hiding places. The players need a circle about 5 feet in diameter. In the middle, they place an empty can. One player is chosen as It, and he stands in the circle guarding the can, while the rest of the players stand outside the circle. When a player thinks he can catch It off-guard, he runs into the circle and kicks the can as far as possible. While It runs after the can, the rest of the players run for cover. When It retrieves the can, and gets it back to the circle, he yells "Freeze!" and all players have to stop in their tracks. It can now call the names of any players in sight. They become prisoners and have to stand with one foot in the circle. Meanwhile, It can leave the circle, trying to capture the remaining players.

If It gets far enough away, one of those players can run to the circle and kick the can. This frees all prisoners, who can run and hide while It retrieves the can. If there are no prisoners, one player can run for the circle and if he makes it before It catches him, he yells "Home Free!" All players, including It, may then run for the circle. The last one to the circle becomes It for the next round.

16 Lions and Antelopes

Best for Ages: 5 and up

Number of Players Required: 3 or more

Equipment Needed: None

How to Play: One of the players is selected to be the Lion. An area of the playing field is designated as the Lion's den. The rest of the players are the Antelopes. The Antelopes have their own home base — away from the Lion's den — where they're safe from capture. The game starts with the Lion in his den. The Antelopes approach the den in a straight line, but spaced as far apart as possible. At any time, the Lion can rush out of his den and chase an Antelope. If the Lion tags an Antelope away from home base, that player goes into the Lion's den. The remaining Antelopes return to their starting point, and once again approach the Lion's den. When only one Antelope is left, that player becomes the Lion and the game starts over.

17 Puss in the Corner

Best for Ages: 5 and up

Number of Players Required: 5

Equipment Needed: None

How to Play: Four players make a square, one at each corner. The fifth player is Puss, who stands in the middle, hoping to take over a corner during the game. The players at the corners have to change places during the game. They can call or signal to each other, trying to get to another corner before Puss can. If Puss has trouble getting a corner, she can yell, "All switch!" Each player has to head for another corner, and if Puss makes it to a corner, the player who's left out goes in the middle and becomes Puss for the next game.

18 Ring-a-Levio

Best for Ages: 7 and up

Number of Players Required: 2 teams of 3 or more

Equipment Needed: None

How to Play: This is a fast-action, rough-and-tumble game. The two sides mark off a jail, big enough so that all players from one team can stand inside it. One team is chosen as It. As the members of the It team count to 100 by fives, the other team members scatter for cover. When finished counting, the It team announces: "Ready or not, here we come!" All members of the It team try to capture the other players. The It team leaves one player behind to guard the jail. The jailer must keep one foot in the jail at all times. When members of the It team capture an opposing player, they have to say "Ring-a-Levio, 1,2,3!" three times. The player can escape, however, if he gets loose from the It team member before she can say this. Captured players have to be brought to jail. They can break out of jail if a teammate tags them. Captured players can try to push the jailer out of the jail or pull him in. Any time the jailer doesn't have one foot in and one foot outside the jail, the captured players can escape. When the It team captures all the opposing players, the game is over and the teams change sides.

19 Sardines

Best for Ages: 5 and up
Number of Players Required: 2 to 8
Equipment Needed: None
How to Play: This game is Hide and Seek in reverse. A backyard with plenty of hiding places is the ideal playing ground. One player is chosen as It, and the rest cover their eyes and count to 20. While the others count, It finds a roomy place to hide. The rest of the players try to find him. When a player finds It's hiding place, she doesn't say anything to the rest. Instead, she waits until no one's looking and hides with It. The rest of the players do likewise, and the hiding place becomes packed, like a can of sardines. The game continues until the last player finds the hiding place. The first player to find the hiding spot takes over as It for the next round.

20 Search Party

Best for Ages: 7 and up

Number of Players Required: 2 teams of 3 or more

Equipment Needed: None

How to Play: A good-size area, with lots of hiding places, works best. After marking an area as base camp, the players form two teams of equal number. One group is the Hikers, the other group is the Search Party. The Hikers leave base camp, while the Search Party remains. Along the way, the Hikers pick one player who will get "lost" on the hike. This player will not return with the rest of the Hikers. When the Hikers return to base camp, the Searchers have to figure out which player is missing. The Searchers go to look for the lost Hiker, who tries to evade the Search Party. The rest of the Hikers remain at home base. If the lost Hiker makes it back to base camp without being caught, he chooses one player from the Search Party to become a Hiker. If the Searchers catch the lost Hiker, he becomes part of the Search Party. The players then change sides. The game continues until one side has no players left.

Playing Tip:

★ If possible, Search Party should be played over several connecting backyards.

21 Shadow Tag

Best for Ages: 5 and up
Number of Players Required: 3 or more
Equipment Needed: None
How to Play: This game, which originated in Japan, is the opposite of Flashlight Tag. It requires a sunny day. "It" chases the other players, and when he steps on someone's shadow, that player becomes "It."

Playing tips:

★ Players should keep far apart to keep their shadows from overlapping.
★ The time of day is an important factor in Shadow Tag. Shadows are longer at sunset and toward evening than they are at midday.

22 Smear the Quarterback

Best for Ages: 12 and up

Number of Players Required: 3 or more

Equipment Needed: Large ball (soccer or football)

How to Play: The most rough-and-tumble tag game, Smear the Quarterback is not for the faint-hearted! Any number of players, 12 or older, can take part. But the more participants, the better the game. The only requirements are a sizeable yard and a large ball — a soccer ball or football will do. The game starts when one player throws the ball in any direction, and all players run toward it. The player who picks up the ball becomes the Quarterback. The Quarterback runs with the ball while the other players try to tag him. The Quarterback runs for as long as he can without being tagged. If the Quarterback is about to be tagged, he throws the ball away. Whoever picks up the ball becomes the Quarterback. If the Quarterback is tagged while holding the ball, the game starts over.

23 Squat Tag

Best for Ages: 5 and up

Number of Players Required: 5 to 10

Equipment Needed: None

How to Play: When It comes near a player, that player can squat to avoid being tagged. This means It has to be a little more crafty when trying to tag another player.

Playing tip:

★ In order to tag another player, It really has to use his or her wits in this version. The best way to tag an opponent is to chase one player, then quickly change direction to catch another player off guard. Sneaking up on other players is also recommended.

24 TV Tag

Best for Ages: 7 and up

Number of Players Required: 3 or more

Equipment Needed: None

How to Play: In the version of the backyard classic, there is no base. Instead, It chases players who try to avoid being tagged. Any player can be safe from It by kneeling on the ground and, at the same time, saying the name of a television show.

PART 2:
Ball Games

25 Around the World

Best for Ages: 7 and up

Number of Players Required: 2 to 5

Equipment Needed: Chalk, a basketball and a court area

How to Play: This game helps develop shooting skills for young basketball players. On the court, the players mark off seven "shot spots" with chalk or tape. The shot spots should form a semicircle, no closer than 12-20 feet to the hoop, depending on the players' ages and skill. The players choose a shooting order. The first player shoots from the first shot spot. If she makes it, she moves to the second shot spot. The shooter continues until she misses. Then it's the second shooter's turn. The players continue until it's the first shooter's turn again. The first shooter resumes play from the last spot she missed. The first player to go Around the World — hitting a shot from each shot spot — is the winner.

26 Box Baseball

Best for Ages: 7 and up

Number of Players Required: 2

Equipment Needed: Chalk and a playground ball

How to Play: It can be played across three sidewalk squares or on a driveway with three boxes of equal size drawn in chalk. Each player picks a team and writes the team name inside one of the outside boxes. The box in the center is the strike zone. The players face each other, each standing behind their team's box. One player tosses the ball over the strike zone into the other player's box. The other player tries to catch the ball on one bounce. If he does, it's an out. If he doesn't, each additional bounce the ball takes is one base. Five bounces equals a home run. If the player's throw lands in the strike zone or outside the other team's box, it counts as a strike. Three strikes equal one out. Three outs end an inning, and 9 innings constitute one game.

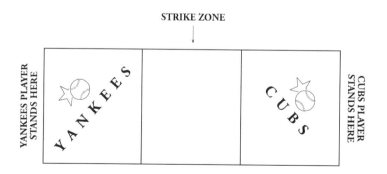

27 Catch-a-Fly, You're Up

Best for Ages: 7 and up

Number of Players Required: 3 or more

Equipment Needed: A tennis ball and a bat

How to Play: One player takes a bat and a ball, tosses the ball into the air and then hits to the other players. Any player who catches a fly ball or a line drive gets to bat.

Playing tips:

★ Soft balls, like a tennis ball, don't require a baseball glove and work best for younger players. Fielders can line up in the field as in baseball, but with no catcher or pitcher. If there are more than two players at the same position, they must be at least double arms' length apart.

Variations:

Any fielder who makes three catches of ground balls off the same batter gets a turn at bat.

28 Dodge Ball

Best for Ages: 7 and up

Number of Players Required: 2 teams of 6 or more

Equipment Needed: A large, soft ball like a volleyball or kickball

How to Play: The players must be equally divided between the two teams. One team forms a large circle. Inside this circle, the other team gathers in a smaller circle. For a designated time period (usually 2-4 minutes), the outside team has the ball and gets to throw it at players on the opposite team. The team with the ball can pass before shooting. Any player hit by the ball is out. Players on the outside team can only throw at members of the opposing team while in their circle. Outside players may leave their circle to retrieve the ball, but can't throw until they're back in the circle. After the time period is up, the two teams change sides, with the players from the inside circle changing places with the remaining players on the outside circle. This continues until all players from one team are eliminated.

Playing tips:

★ Players can aim the ball only below an opponent's waist. A player isn't out when the ball hits him above the waist.

Variation:

Instead of forming circles, the two teams face each other in equal-sized squares. Neither side can cross over the center line, and there are no time limits. Whoever recovers the ball gets to throw it.

29 Elephant Ball

Best for Ages: 7 and up

Number of Players Required: 2

Equipment Needed: A bat and a basketball

How to Play: This game has more in common with track and field jumping and throwing events than with traditional ball games. There are no bases in Elephant Ball. The positions are Batter and Pitcher. Both players get a turn at bat, and each turn at bat consists of six swings. The object is for the Batter to hit the ball as far as possible. The longest hit for each player is marked, either with the player's hat or his baseball glove. The player with the longest hit is the winner.

Playing tips:

★ The Pitcher throws underhand, as in softball, and doesn't try to fool the batter.

★ The Pitcher tries to catch batted balls, either on the fly or on the ground.

★ The Pitcher marks the spot where he catches or stops the ball. If a ball gets past the Pitcher, the spot where it stops rolling is marked. Because of the size and weight of a basketball, it's hard to hit it past the Pitcher. Almost any ball hit beyond the pitcher is an automatic game-winner!

30 Five Hundred

Best for Ages: 5 and up

Number of Players Required: 3 or more

Equipment Needed: A tennis ball

How to Play: There are no set number of players in this game, but the more the merrier. One person is chosen as the Thrower, and everyone else lines up if front of him as a Catcher. The Thrower tosses the ball in the air, and each of the players try to catch it. As he tosses the ball, the Thrower calls out a number. Whoever catches the ball earns that many points. Players must catch the ball in the air, not on a bounce, to score points. The first player to reach 500 points wins and gets a turn as the Thrower.

Playing tips:

★ This game is even more fun if the Catchers are in a backyard pool, and the Thrower is on solid ground. It can also be played as a beach game, with the Catchers in the surf and the Thrower on the sand.

Variations:

After tossing the ball in the air, the Thrower can yell "Poison!" Any player who catches the ball after a "Poison" call loses her points. The Thrower can also yell "Surprise" while the ball is in the air. If a player catches the ball on a "Surprise" call, the Thrower can designate a bonus (up to 200 points) for that Catcher, or call Poison, which results in the loss of all points. The Thrower can also yell "Jackpot," and the player who catches the ball on that call earns an automatic 500 points and becomes the Thrower.

31 Flag Football

Best for Ages: 7 and up

Number of Players Required: 2 teams of 3 or more

Equipment Needed: A football, 2 strips of cloth or hand-kerchiefs for each player

How to Play: This game is played just like football, but with one big difference: no tackling. Instead, players wear two small flags. One end of the flags (which can be strips of cloth or handkerchiefs) is tucked into belts or pockets. Flags must be visible and can't be tied on. Defensive players stop a ball carrier by taking both his flags. Other than that, football playing rules are in effect.

32 Four Square

Best for Ages: 7 and up

Number of Players Required: 4 or more

Equipment Needed: A large, bouncy ball, such as a kickball and tape or chalk to mark out the court

How to Play: After diagramming a square of about 3 feet by 3 feet, divide that square into four more squares of 18 inches by 18 inches. One player goes into each square; any additional players remain on deck, waiting their turn. One player is chosen King, and his square is designated as Square One. Moving clockwise, the players and their squares are numbered two through four. The King gets to declare whether this round of Four Square will be a basic game or one of the variants. The players line up on the outside corners of their squares. Play starts when the King bounces the ball on Square One and then taps it to another player's square. After the first bounce, that player has to tap the ball to another player's square.

Play continues until:
* ★ a player fails to tap the ball after one bounce
* ★ a player taps the ball so it lands on a line
* ★ a player taps the ball back onto his own space.

When a player goes out, the others (except for the King) rotate clockwise to fill the empty space and one of the on-deck players moves onto the fourth square. If the King goes out, the player in Square Two rotates into Square One and becomes King. Any time a player goes out, the action stops until the players rotate and a new player moves into the Fourth Square. Spiking the ball is an automatic disqualification. This game continues indefinitely, ending when the players decide to try another game, or it's time to go home.

Variations:

The King can declare that each player is allowed two "bobbles" — that is, the players have to juggle the ball twice before tapping it to another square. Bobbling the ball helps a player to keep the other players on their toes while the player with the ball decides where to tap it.

33 Home Run Derby

Best for Ages: 7 and up

Number of Players Required: 2

Equipment Needed: A bat, ball and glove

How to Play: Back in the 1950s, "Home Run Derby" was a popular television show featuring major league baseball sluggers who would match up in home run-hitting contests. When the show began airing on cable TV in the 1990s, a new generation of baseball fans saw it and started playing this simple version of baseball. This game needs just two players, a hitter and a pitcher who switch sides after three outs, just as in regular baseball. Anyone else who wants to play can wait his turn and, in the meantime, retrieve batted balls. They should also have a large playing area, with no chance for a batted ball to smash a window or anything else breakable. A fence in the outfield is also helpful. The rules are simple: anything hit over the wall is a homer and earns the batter a run. Anything else is an out. Any pitched ball outside the strike zone doesn't count. The player with the most runs wins.

34 Horse

Best for Ages: 7 and up

Number of Players Required: 2 to 5

Equipment Needed: A basketball and a basketball goal

How to Play: Players choose a shooting order. The first player names a shot — a hook shot from the foul line, for example — and, if he makes it, each player has to duplicate that shot. Any player who misses gets the letter "H". If the first player makes his shot, he leads off again and makes another shot, usually one more difficult than the first. Again, the rest of the players have to match the shot. If the first player calls his shot and misses, the second shooter gets to name the shot. Any player who spells "H-O-R-S-E' with five misses is out. When only one shooter is left, that player is the winner.

35 Kickball

Best for Ages: 7 and up
Number of Players Required: 2 teams of 4-9 players
Equipment Needed: A kickball
How to Play: In many elementary schools, Kickball is an organized sport and, in most areas, kickballs are produced commercially and available in stores. A kickball is large, soft, usually brick red in color, and very bouncy. The game is played on a field set up like a scaled-down baseball or softball diamond (anywhere from 45 to 60 feet between bases), with players lining up at the usual positions (pitcher, catcher, first base, etc.). Baseball rules apply, with one major difference: the pitcher rolls the ball toward home plate, and the "batter" tries to kick it between the opposing players. Teams can play for a set number of innings, and the side with the most runs wins.

36 Monkey in the Middle

Best for Ages: 7 and up

Number of Players Required: 5 or more

Equipment Needed: A ball or beanbag

How to Play: One player is chosen as the Monkey and stands between the other players. The other players line up 15-20 feet apart (farther for older players). The first player in one line tries to throw the ball to the first player in the other line. If that player is successful, he runs to the back of the opposite line. This continues until the Monkey intercepts a throw or picks up a dropped ball. When that happens, the player who threw the ball becomes the Monkey in the Middle. This game is also known as Keepaway.

37 One-Old-Cat

Best for Ages: 7 and up

Number of Players Required: 2 or more

Equipment Needed: A bat, 2 bases and a soft ball

How to Play: The playing field requires two bases about 50-70 feet apart. With two players, the batter hits the ball out of his hand and runs from one base to another until his opponent is close enough to tag him off base. Each time a player touches the base he batted from, he scores a run. The batter is retired when the fielder catches the ball on the fly or on one bounce, or tags the runner off-base. The number of players can be increased by playing "two-," "three-" or "four-old-cat," by adding to the number of bases and players. Although rarely played today, One-Old-Cat is an ancestor of modern-day baseball.

38 Popcorn

Best for Ages: 9 and up
Number of Players Required: 4 or more
Equipment Needed: A volleyball
How to Play: Players divide into teams of two or three.
Each group must have a volleyball. Teams should give
one another plenty of space. The game begins when one
player sets the ball, and his teammates keep it going. A
player may not set the ball twice in a row. Any time a
ball hits the ground, the team is out. The last team still
going is the winner.

39 Punchball

Best for Ages: 9 and up
Number of Players Required: 2 teams of 4 to 9 players
Equipment Needed: A soft rubber ball
How to Play: Here's a backyard ballgame guaranteed
not to break any windows. Players map out home plate
and 4 bases, and they divide into two equal teams. Punch
ball doesn't require a pitcher. Each "batter" tosses a soft,
rubber ball into the air, just like a tennis player does when
serving. With a clenched fist, the batter tries to hit the
ball so that it lands safely. Usual baseball or softball rules
apply: any ball caught on a fly is an out; any grounder
fielded and thrown to a base before a runner arrives is
an out; if a batter doesn't hit a fair ball in three tries,
that's a strikeout.

40 Queenie

Best for Ages: 5 and up

Number of Players Required: 4 to 12

Equipment Needed: A small rubber ball

How to Play: One player is chosen as It, or Queenie. While the other players stand in a circle, Queenie turns her back and throws the ball over her head and into the circle. When one of the players catches the ball, the players get back into the circle, facing Queenie, and stand with their hands behind their backs. When everyone's in place, they all say "Ready." Queenie has to turn around and guess which player is hiding the ball. If she's right, she has another turn as Queenie. If she's wrong, the player who has the ball becomes Queenie.

41 Soccer Baseball

Best for Ages: 9 and up

Number of Players Required: 2 teams of 5 or more

Equipment Needed: A soccer ball.

How to Play: Soccer Baseball combines the skills and playing rules of these two sports. Players divide into two equal teams and map out first, second and third base, plus home plate. The defensive team takes its positions. With only 5 players, one player is the pitcher (and also covers home plate); another is an outfielder, and the other three cover each base. If there are more than 9 players on a side, defensive players can line up anywhere. Just like soccer, no one can touch the ball with their hands. The pitcher kicks the ball toward the batter. There are no balls and strikes. The batter tries to kick the ball wherever the pitcher places it (but the pitcher does try to get it over home plate). Once a batter kicks the ball, he runs all around the bases without stopping. The fielders — without using their hands — try to get the batter out.

There's a major rule difference, however, between baseball and Soccer Baseball: if the batter gets past first base, the fielders have to get the ball to each base — in order — to retire him. For example: the batter kicks the ball into the outfield. No matter where the batter is, the outfielder kicks the ball to first base. Even if the batter is around second by then, the first baseman kicks the ball to the second baseman. If the batter is rounding third, the second baseman still has to kick the ball to third before the third baseman can boot it home in an attempt to get the batter out. Fielders may come off the bag to retrieve the ball. If the batter circles the bases, that counts as a run. If the batter is retired at any base or at home plate, that's one out. Regular baseball rules apply: the side is retired after three outs, games go nine innings, and the team with the most runs wins.

42 Soccer Golf

Best for Ages: 7 and up
Number of Players Required: 2 or more
Equipment Needed: A soccer ball
How to Play: This game is like miniature golf... but with a soccer ball. The "golfers" lay out a course in the backyard. Each "hole" is indicated by some kind of marker (a strip of cardboard, a cloth, etc. The holes should be spread out along the course. The players then kick the ball toward the first hole. Players keep track of the number of kicks it takes to reach the hole. After all holes have been played, the player with the lowest score wins.

43 Spud

Best for Ages: 5 and up

Number of Players Required: 2 to 6

Equipment Needed: A kickball

How to Play: Each player secretly picks a number from 1 to 10. After the players choose their number, they form a circle. One player throws the ball in the air, calling a number between 1 and 10 (it can't be a number that the player has chosen for himself). Any player who hears her number called — there may be more than one — must try to catch the ball. When the player gets the ball, he yells "Spud," and every player has to freeze on the spot. The player with the ball is allowed 10 steps in the direction of the player closest to her. On her final step, the player with the ball gets to throw it at the nearest opponent. The player she throws at can try to avoid contact by ducking or jumping — but he can't move forward or backward, or from side to side. A player who is hit by the throw gets an 'S'; a player who throws and misses acquires the 'S.' Any player who gets the letters S, P, U and D is out. The last player remaining is the winner.

44 Stoop Ball

Best for Ages: 9 and up

Number of Players Required: 5

Equipment Needed: A set of steps (brick or concrete) and a rubber ball (or tennis ball)

How to Play: The "batter" stands at least a foot or two from the bottom step. The first baseman stands 8-10 feet behind him, followed by the second baseman, the third baseman and the outfielder. How far back these fielders play is determined by the amount of space available.

★ The batter throws the ball against the steps as hard as he can.

★ A ground ball fielded by the first baseman is a strike.

★ A grounder fielded by the second baseman is a single.

★ A grounder fielded by the third baseman is a double.

★ Any grounder fielded by the outfielder is a triple.

★ On each hit, the imaginary runners move up accordingly on the base paths.

★ Any ball that sails over the outfielder's head is a home run.

★ When a fielder catches a fly ball, the batter is out and changes place with that fielder.

★ If a batter strikes out, he moves to the outfield and all players move up.

The winner is the first player to reach a predetermined number of runs or the player with the highest score when it's time to go inside.

45 Ten Again

Best for Ages: 7 and up
Number of Players Required: 5 or more
Equipment Needed: A soccer ball
How to Play: Similar to Dodgeball, in Ten Again one player is chosen as It, and the rest of the players form a circle. It goes into the center, and the other players get 10 chances to kick the ball at her. If It gets hit by a kicked ball, the player who kicked the ball becomes It. If It survives all 10 kicks, she gets another turn in the middle. Players may pass the ball to another player in order to get a better shot, but must yell "Pass." Passes do not count as one of the ten shots. And, if It gets hit on a pass, she still continues in the middle.

46 Twenty-One

Best for Ages: 9 and up
Number of Players Required: 2 or more
Equipment Needed: A basketball, some chalk and a goal
How to Play: The players draw an arc around where the free-throw line would be. The players decide a shooting order, and the first shooter takes a shot from behind the line. It's a 3-pointer if he sinks it. If he misses, he gets his own rebound and shoots from that point. If the ball goes in, it's 2 points. His next shot is a layup, worth a point. This gives the shooter a chance for 6 points every turn. Each of the other players repeats the process. The object is to score exactly 21 points. Any player starting his turn with 20 points has to miss his first two shots and try for the layup. Any player who goes over 21 loses all his points and goes back to zero.

PART 3:
Group Action Games

47 All the Fish in the Sea

Best for Ages: 5 and up

Number of Players Required: 16 to 40

Equipment Needed: None

How to Play: One player is chosen as Caller. The rest sit around in a large circle. The Caller walks around the circle, assigning each player to a group of fish — shark, sailfish, barracuda, swordfish, etc. Each group needs about 8-10 players. When the Caller says, "Sharks are swimming," all the players designated as sharks get up and run clockwise around the circle and return to their places. The last player standing is out, and has to stand in place. When the Caller says, "All the fish in the sea are swimming," all players get up and run clockwise around the circle, and return to their places. Again, the last player standing is out and stands in place. As often as possible, the Caller says, "Tide's turning," and the players have to change direction. The game continues until only one player is left.

48 Balloon Race

Best for Ages: 7 and up

Number of Players Required: 6 or more

Equipment Needed: two balloons, two pieces of cardboard and some string

How to Play: This is one of the slowest relay races. The players are divided into two teams. Each team has a balloon with a string attached at the end, and a piece of cardboard. At the command "Go," the first players from each team toss the balloons in the air. Using the cardboard as a fan, each player tries to keep her balloon airborne as she runs from the starting line to another point about 20 feet away. At this turning point, the players — still keeping the balloons in the air — have to turn around and return to the starting line. There, the first player passes the cardboard to the next player in line, who repeats the process. The first team to successfully get the balloon back and forth without letting it touch the ground is the winner.

49 Blindman's Buff

Best for Ages: 5 and up

Number of Players Required: 8 or more

Equipment Needed: A blindfold

How to Play: Over the years, the name of this game seems to have evolved into Blindman's Bluff. But the correct word in this game's title is "buff" — meaning blow or buffet — a term, now obsolete, that indicates the game's origins between the 11th and 14th centuries. One of the players is chosen as It. The other players tie a blindfold over It's eyes and turn him around three times. Then they form a circle, facing inward, holding hands and skipping counterclockwise. At any time, It may call "stop," and when he does, everyone stands in place. Then, It points and the player closest to his finger enters the circle. That player tries to avoid being tagged by It. If tagged, It gets to touch the player's face, and tries to guess the player's identity. If It guesses correctly, he changes places with that player.

Variation:

In an older version more similar to tag, the players do not stand in a circle. After It gets spun around three times, he tries to catch one of the players. They can tease It by pulling at his clothes or tickling his face with a feather. Only when It catches a player does he get to guess their identity. The name of the game derives from this ancient, rougher version, since participants could "buffet" the blindfolded It.

50 Cat and Mouse

Best for Ages: 5 and up

Number of Players Required: 6 or more

Equipment Needed: None

How to Play: One player is selected as the Cat, while another is designated as the Mouse. The remaining players form a circle, holding hands. The Cat goes outside the circle, while the mouse goes inside and announces, "I am the Mouse, and you can't catch me!" To which the Cat answers: "I am the Cat! We'll see, we'll see!" The Cat tries to catch the Mouse, and the players in the circle try to help the Mouse avoid the Cat. If the Cat tries to enter the circle, they hold hands to keep him out, while they drop their hands to let the Mouse out of the circle. When the Mouse is caught, she joins the circle. The Cat becomes the new Mouse, and another player is chosen to be the Cat.

51 Chicken Fight

Best for Ages: 10 and up

Number of Players Required: 4 or more

Equipment Needed: None

How to Play: Smaller players get onto the shoulders of the bigger players, and the object of the game is to topple each of the other teams. Only players on top can use their hands.

Playing tip:

★ Chicken Fights are great in pools or at the beach.

52 Circle Ball Race

Best for Ages: 5 and up

Number of Players Required: 2 teams of 5-10 players

Equipment Needed: 2 balls

How to Play: Players divide into two teams of equal size and select a captain. Both teams will need a ball. Each team forms a circle, with each of the players standing apart the same distance. The object of the game is to be the first team to pass the ball around the circle five times. Players have several options. They can elect to throw the ball the first time around; kick the ball the second time around; bounce the ball the third time around; roll the ball the ball the fourth time around; and throw the ball once again on the fifth time around (any combination is acceptable, as long as both teams follow the pattern). Play begins at the command "Go," and each team captain passes the ball to the player on her right. Each time the ball gets back to the team captain, she says "one," "two," etc., and the first to reach five wins.

53 Cops and Smugglers

Best for Ages: 5 and up
Number of Players Required: 2 teams of 2 or more
Equipment Needed: Coins, stones or hairpins
How to Play: One group is the Cops, the other the Smugglers. The Cops have a home base, while the Smugglers have a small object (coin, stone, hairpin) that serves as the Jewel. While the Cops gather at home base and start to count, the Smugglers start moving away. When the Cops get to 50, they yell "Smugglers!" and start to chase the other team. One Smuggler carries the jewel, which he can pass to other Smugglers to confuse the Cops. Any Smuggler tagged must open his hands. When a Smuggler is caught with the Jewel, the teams change sides.

Playing tip:

★ Smugglers should try to confuse the Cops by passing off the Jewel. Smugglers should also try to decoy the Cops by pretending to pass the Jewel to teammates.

Variation:

When Cops catch a Smuggler without the Jewel, they put him in prison at home base. The Smuggler with the Jewel, however, can free a teammate in prison if he can pass the Jewel to him.

54 Crack the Whip

Best for Ages: 9 and up
Number of Players Required: 6 or more
Equipment Needed: 2 balls
How to Play: This should be played on a soft, grassy playing surface or on snow. The players get in line and hold hands tightly, with the biggest, strongest player at the end of the line. At the command "Go," the players start running. After they reach top speed, the player at the end of the line "cracks the whip" by stopping suddenly. When the whip cracks, the players at the end of the line go flying.

55 Dizzy Bat Race

Best for Ages: 3 and up
Number of Players Required: 2 or more
Equipment Needed: 2 baseball bats
How to Play: The hilarious Dizzy Bat Race is a popular between-innings sideshow at many minor league baseball parks. Players decide on start and finish lines. Each player takes a baseball bat and goes to the starting line. Placing the bat straight up and down, the players bend over and touch the tip of the bat with their foreheads. The players then run around as quickly as possible, keeping the bat in the same position and never losing contact with their foreheads. After five turns, the dizzy players drop their bats and begin stumbling toward the finish line. The first one there is the winner.

56 Follow the Leader

Best for Ages: 5 and up

Number of Players Required: 4 or more

Equipment Needed: None

How to Play: One player is chosen as the Leader, who stands in the front of the line. The players follow the Leader around, making all the movements she makes. If the Leader marches in place, the players do the same; if the Leader skips, the players skip, etc. Any player who fails to imitate the Leader's movements is out. Playing tips: This game works best if a new leader is chosen after a set amount of time.

Variations:

Players line up in a semicircle, holding hands. The leader stands in front of the group. In this version, the Leader touches his nose, pats his stomach, etc., and the players follow suit. Any time a player does not follow the leader, he changes places with the player on his left. Any player who reaches the end of the line is out.

57 Frisbee Golf

Best for Ages: 9 and up
Number of Players Required: 2 or more
Equipment Needed: Frisbee
How to Play: Here's another version of golf, one that doesn't require greens fees, clubs or even a ball, just a lot of imagination. The players designate a tee-off area anywhere in the middle of the yard. Next, they designate "holes" — an object like a mailbox, tree, dog house, telephone pole, basketball goal —anything that can serve as a target for the frisbee. Each player tosses the frisbee at the hole. If the frisbee touches the object on the first toss, the player scores a hole-in-one. If not, that player goes to the spot where the frisbee landed and tries again. Players keep throwing until the frisbee touches the hole. Players keep count of how many tosses it takes them to reach the hole. The player with the lowest score wins. Players can play as many holes as they can devise.

Playing tips:

★ If they chose, players can agree upon a par for each hole (mailbox is a par 2; dog house is a par 3, etc.). They can also elect to designate areas of the backyard as sand traps or water hazards. For example, the driveway can be a water hazard, and a sand box can do double duty as a sand trap. Landing on a sand trap or a water hazard adds one stroke to a player's score for that hole.

58 I Declare War

Best for Ages: 7 and up

Number of Players Required: 5 to 10

Equipment Needed: 1 ball and some chalk

How to Play: The players need a good-sized section of driveway, plus plenty of space. First, the players draw a circle. Next, they draw a larger, concentric circle. This part of the two circles is divided into equal parts, one for each player. Each of these sections is marked with the name of a country of each player's choice. The game begins with one player standing on his "country." That player says, "I declare war on Canada (or Mexico, or Venezuela, or any other player's country)," and throws the ball with all his might straight down into the middle of the smaller circle. If the player declares war on Canada, that player has to freeze, while all the other players run from the circle. When the ball comes down, Canada tries to retrieve the ball. As soon as Canada has the ball, he yells "Freeze!" and the players stop running. Canada may then take three giant steps toward any other player. Canada can then try to hit that player with the ball. If Canada hits the player, that player must then declare war in the next round. If Canada misses, all players can run back to their "country" and Canada again has to declare war.

59 Johnny on the Pony

Best for Ages: 10 and up

Number of Players Required: 2 teams of 4 or more

Equipment Needed: A fire hydrant, a tree or a pole

How to Play: After choosing sides, the teams flip a coin. The losing team has to bend over in a line, each with his arms around the waist of the player in front of him to create the "Pony." The first player in line puts his arms around the fire hydrant, tree, etc. One by one, the opposing team, the Johnny, jumps on the backs of the Pony. As they try to move forward toward the tree, pole or hydrant, they try to break the Pony. If the Pony stays intact after all members of the Johnny team are on, they win. If the members of the Pony get separated, the other team wins. Playing tip: The members of the Pony team can try to shake off the members of the Johnny team, as long as they don't separate from their teammates. The Johnny team, of course, does whatever it can to make the Pony players break apart.

60 Leapfrog

Best for Ages: 5 and up

Number of Players Required: 2 or more

Equipment Needed: None

How to Play: Leapfrog requires one player to leap over her playmates while they stand in line about five or six feet apart, bent over with hands touching ankles. When the leaper reaches the end of the line, she becomes the front end of the line and bends down. Then the last player in line stands up and starts jumping over the other players. With enough players, leapfrog can be a racing contest. Divide the players into even numbered teams. At the command "Go," the players at the back of both lines begin jumping over their teammates. The winning team is either the one that reaches a finish line first, or the one that's the first to have everyone complete their jumps.

61 London Bridge

Best for Ages: 3 and up

Number of Players Required: 8 to 10

Equipment Needed: None

How to Play: Two players face each other and join hands, arms raised above their heads. Through this arch, or "bridge," the other players pass in a continuous circle, holding hands. All the while, the players sing: *London Bridge is falling down, falling down, falling down. London Bridge is falling down, my fair lady.*

On last word of the song, the bridge comes down as the two players drop their arms. Whichever player is caught is out of the game, and the players sing: *Take the key and lock him up, lock him up, lock him up. Take the key and lock him up, my fair lady.* A variation of this verse is: *Off to prison he must go, he must go, he must go. Off to prison he must go, my fair lady.* The last player not caught is the winner.

Variation:

The two players who form the bridge are chosen as Leaders, each with a secret identity — one as an Angel, the other as a Devil. When the bridge falls and a player is captured, that player chooses which Leader he or she will follow. When the game ends, the Leaders disclose their identities, and the players learn which side they've selected — Good or Evil. The Leader with the most followers is the winner. Instead of Good and Evil, the Leaders can choose to be animals (tigers or bears, for example), colors (red or blue) or sports teams (Knicks or Pacers).

62 Marbles

Best for Ages: 7 and up
Number of Players Required: 2 or more
Equipment Needed: Marbles and chalk
How to Play: Like almost all low-tech pastimes, the ancient game of Marbles has been all but ignored in recent years. Decades ago, however, marbles were as much a harbinger of spring as the first robin or baseball. In its simplest version, Marbles can be played on dirt or a driveway. The players mark off a starting line. The first player shoots his marble from behind the line. The next player attempts to hit the first player's marble with his shot. If he does, the second player wins the first player's marble. If he misses, the next player tries for either marble. (In a two-player game, the first player gets to shoot at the two marbles in play.) When a player's shot hits a marble, he can continue shooting at any marbles still in play. If it's a player's turn and there are no marbles in play, that player then shoots his marble just as the lead off player did, and the game continues. The player who accrues the greatest number of marbles is the winner.

63 Marbles Baseball

Best for Ages: 7 and up

Number of Players Required: 2

Equipment Needed: Marbles and chalk

How to Play: This game requires a flat playing surface, like a driveway or sidewalk. On an area about the size of one sidewalk square, players mark off a smaller square in each corner. The square in the lower left-hand and right-hand corners are marked "single." The upper right-hand corner is marked "double, and the upper left-hand corner is marked "triple." A circle between the two upper squares is marked "home run." Players decide who "bats" first. Kneeling about three feet from the playing surface, the "batter" tries to roll a marble onto one of the squares or the circle. Anything that lands outside the squares or circle is an out. The game goes 9 innings, and whoever has the most runs is the winner.

64 Mother, May I?

Best for Ages: 5 and up

Number of Players Required: 3 or more

Equipment Needed: None

How to Play: One player is selected as Mother. The rest line up around 20 feet away, all in a row. From left to right and one at a time, Mother calls each player by name and gives them instructions as to how many steps they can take. For example, the Mother may call out: "Nancy, you may take two giant steps forward." Nancy has to respond, "Mother, may I?" If she does not, she has to return to the starting line. If she does, Mother can say "Yes, you may," or, "No you may not," or even "No you may not, instead take two baby steps." Again, before making a move, the player must ask: "Mother, may I?" Any player who fails to ask "Mother, may I?" at any point has to go back to the starting line. The first player to cross the imaginary line where Mother is standing is the winner.

Playing tip:

★ The player chosen as Mother should mix up the number and type of steps.

65 Musical Stones

Best for Ages: 5 and up
Number of Players Required: 5 or more
Equipment Needed: Stones/rocks
How to Play: Musical Chairs, one of the most popular indoor games, can be converted to an outdoor pastime by substituting stones for seats. The players sit in a circle, facing outward. If there are eight players, there are just seven stones in play. The music starts, and the players begin passing the stones clockwise, behind their backs. When the music stops, the player who doesn't have a stone is out. One stone is then withdrawn, and the game continues until only one player is left. That player is the winner.

66 Pro Flip

Best for Ages: 7 and up

Number of Players Required: 3 or more

Equipment Needed: Pennies and assorted odds-and-ends to make a course

How to Play: Any number of players can take part in this golf spin-off. One player is designated as the Pro, and all players must have a penny. The Pro determines the course, which can consist of a cup, a sheet of paper, an unused flower pot, a baseball cap, etc. One at a time, the players toss their pennies at the object. Any coin that lands in or on the object is a hole in one. To determine the score for each hole, players measure the distance of their pennies from the hole. The closest scores a 2; the next farthest scores a 3, etc. The player with the lowest score is the winner.

Playing Tips:

★ Using hard substances like a can or a dish works best, since players can actually hear the sounds of a penny landing on the hole.

★ While a tape measure is helpful to determine distances, players can also use their shoes, belts or even a stick or a piece of rope for measuring.

67 Races

Best for Ages: 5 and up
Number of Players Required: 2 or more
Equipment Needed: None
How to Play: The simplest racing game requires only a starting point and a finish line. Players line up, start running on the command "Go" and try to be the first to cross the finish line. While many race courses are nothing more than a straight line, players can race around the house or make up their own race routes. For relay races, each player runs from the start line to the finish line and back, then tags the next player. A team wins when its last runner is the first to reach the finish line.

Variation:

Players can race as described, but while carrying a cotton ball on a spoon, one-handed. This can also be a relay race.

68 Red Light, Green Light

Best for Ages: 5 and up
Number of Players Required: 4 or more
Equipment Needed: None
How to Play: One player is selected to be the Stoplight.
The others line up at a starting point, about 40 feet away.
Stoplight turns his back to the players. When he calls
out "Green Light," everyone starts running toward him.
Stoplight then yells "Red Light," and all players must
stop and remain motionless. Anyone moving has to go
back to the starting line. The Stoplight continues to call
"Green Light" and "Red Light," varying the pace to
throw off the players. When a player is close enough to
touch Stoplight, these two change places and the game
starts over.

69 Red Rover

Best for Ages: 7 and up
Number of Players Required: 2 teams of 4 or more
Equipment Needed: None
How to Play: The teams face each other, about 10 feet
apart. Holding hands, one team calls a member from the
other team with this chant: "Red Rover, Red Rover, send
Molly right over!" Running at full speed, the player
named must try to break through the ranks of the other
team. If the player succeeds, she gets to bring back to
her own team a player from the opposite side. If the
player doesn't get through, she must join the ranks of
the other team. The game is over when only one player
is left on a team.

70 Simon Says

Best for Ages: 5 and up

Number of Players Required: 3 or more

Equipment Needed: None

How to Play: Here's a game for three or more 5-year-old players. One player is selected to be the Leader, while the rest gather around, facing him — either in a line or a circle. The Leader gestures and gives instructions, which the other players must follow — as long as the directions are preceded by the phrase "Simon Says."

For example, the Leader holds both arms skyward, saying, "Simon Says, hold your arms straight up." The players must follow suit. The Leader may then bend over, saying, "Simon Says, touch your toes," and the players must do likewise. If the Leader then says, "Stand up," anyone who does is out... since the leader didn't say "Simon Says" at the start of the instructions. There are several tricks the Leader can use in trying to fool the players. One is to give instructions very quickly. The other is to instruct the players to do one thing, while making a completely different gesture. The Leader can, for instance, say: "Simon Says, put your hands on your hips," and then place his own hands on his head. Any player who puts her hands on her head is out. The last player left becomes the new Leader.

71 Steal the Bacon

Best for Ages: 7 and up
Number of Players Required: 7 or more
Equipment Needed: Beanbag or something similar
How to Play: One player is selected as the Caller, while the others are divided into two equal teams. Players on either side are given matching numbers, so that there's a "one" on each side, a "two," a "three," etc. The two teams line up about 20 feet apart. The Caller places the Bacon (which can be a beanbag or a can, or even an old hat) between the two teams. When the Caller says a number, the players with that number run toward the Bacon and try to grab it and get it back to their own side without being tagged by the caller. The Caller can announce any number of players, and can play word games to see who's paying attention. For example: "I thought I saw you this morning on Channel 5." At this point, both Number 5 players try to steal the Bacon. "When I play this game, every one knows what to do." Players One and Two must try for the Bacon. "What are you two waiting for?" This signals Players Two and Four into action. Whenever the Caller says the word "Bacon," all players can rush in for a try. The Caller can have fun with the word "Bacon," too. For example: "If anyone plans on bakin' a cake, they can do it right now." This cues the Number 1 players to run into the middle, followed by a signal for everyone to rush in.

72 Tug o' War

Best for Ages: 9 and up

Number of Players Required: 2 teams of 3 or more

Equipment Needed: A sturdy length of rope, 20 feet or more in length

History of the Sport: Here's a backyard game that was once an Olympic event! From 1900 through 1920, Tug of War was contested at the Olympic Games. U.S. tug-of-warriors won a gold medal in 1904 at St. Louis. In fact, with many nations failing to participate, American teams swept the top three places. Tug of War's Olympic history may have been short, but it certainly was controversial.

In 1900 at Paris, the U.S. squad was unable to take part because three of its six members were competing in track and field events. A combined team from Denmark and Sweden defeated the French team for the gold medal. One of the gold medalists was a Danish newspaper reporter who had been a late addition to the team roster.

The 1908 Tug of War at the London Games started one of the biggest controversies in Olympic history. In the first round, a team made up of British policemen from Liverpool easily defeated the American team. The Yanks protested the Bobbies' footgear, claiming it was illegal. The Britons maintained that their steel cleats and spikes were standard police issue, and the protest was denied. The enraged Americans promptly withdrew from the competition. Another British team went on to win the gold medal.

The Brits also won gold in 1920, the last time Tug of War appeared in the Olympics.

How to Play: Backyard Tug o' War is very similar to its Olympic ancestor. Players are divided equally in terms of size and age into two teams. A line is drawn across the center of the playing area. Lining up 3 feet away from either side of the dividing line, players pick up a rope and begin to pull. The first team to drag one of their opponents past the center line is the victor.

73 Ultimate Frisbee

Best for Ages: 12 and up

Number of Players Required: 2 teams of 4 or more

Equipment Needed: Frisbee

How to Play: Patterned after football, Ultimate Frisbee requires a roomy backyard with end zones at either side. The game starts with each team on its own goal line. One team tosses the frisbee to the other side. The offensive team tries to advance to the other team's end zone by passing the frisbee to one another, while the defensive team tries to intercept the frisbee or knock it down. Once a player catches the frisbee, he can't move in any direction until after he tosses to another player. On an incomplete pass, the offensive team loses control of the frisbee. The defensive team then goes on the offense and picks up the frisbee at the point where it landed. Defensive players may guard an opponent, but must stay at least one foot away. A team scores when one player catches the frisbee in the other team's end zone. Each touchdown is worth seven points (there are no extra point attempts). The game can have a time limit, or it can continue until one side accumulates a predetermined number of points.

74 Walk the Plank

Best for Ages: 3 and up

Number of Players Required: 2 or more

Equipment Needed: A rope or tape and binoculars

How to Play: The players lay a 20-foot long rope (or 20 feet of tape) in a straight line. One at a time, the players take the binoculars and, looking through them the wrong way, try to walk the length of the rope.

Playing Tips:

★ Walk the Plank can be made into a contest by determining which player can go the farthest without stepping off the plank.

★ Someone trying to walk while gauging distance through the wrong end of binoculars can be a hilarious spectacle for the other players.

75 Wheelbarrow Race

Best for Ages: 5 and up

Number of Players Required: 4 or more

Equipment Needed: None

How to Play: This is a race in which two players work as partners. At the starting line, one player from each team gets down on all fours. Then his partner picks him up by the ankles. When the race starts, the lead player "runs" on his hands, held up by his partner — who can't go too fast, or his partner will go down. Even if the lead player goes down, however, that team may continue. The first team to the finish is the winner.

PART 4:

Hopping, Jumping & All Sorts of Games

76 Button, Button, Who's Got the Button?

Best for Ages: 5 and up

Number of Players Required: 3 or more

Equipment Needed: A button

How to Play: One player is selected to be It and takes a button (a coin or bottlecap will do in a pinch). The rest of the players sit in a circle, facing inward, with their hands cupped behind their backs. As It walks clockwise around the circle, he pretends to place the button in each player's hand. Even after he actually does give the button to another player, It keeps up the pretense by continuing to go around the circle a few more times. The other players can watch as It goes around, keeping an eye peeled for clues. When It gets back to the center of the circle, he says "Button, button, who's got the button?" Each player takes a turn guessing who has the button. Even the player who does have the button pretends to guess, naming another player in an attempt to fool everyone. The first player to guess gets to be It for the next round.

77 Choosing

Best for Ages: 3 and up

Number of Players Required: 3 or more

Equipment Needed: None

How to Play: Choosing who will be It is an important part of many games. While players often volunteer, sometimes it's necessary to use arbitrary methods to determine who will be It. One of the most common methods is a counting rhyme. One player points to each of the others as she says the rhyme: *Eeenie, meenie, minie, moe. Catch a tiger by the toe. If he hollers, let him go. Eeenie, meenie, minie, moe. My mother said to pick the very best one. Y-O-U spells you.* The player she points to on the final word is chosen as It.

Another method is to have all players stand in a circle, holding out a fist toward the center. One player in the center touches each fist on each word or letter of the following rhyme: *One potato, two potato, three potato, four, five potato, six potato, seven potato more. Y-O-U spells you, And O-U-T spells out.* The player touched on the word out is eliminated, and this continues until one player is left, who becomes It.

Still another way is to play Scissors, Rock, Paper, or to decide by flipping a coin.

78 Four Coin Toss

Best for Ages: 12 and up
Number of Players Required: 3 to 7
Equipment Needed: 4 to 6 pennies and some chalk
How to Play: Four Coin Toss is a very old game, an ancestor of the modern pastime Pitching Pennies. It requires a driveway or sidewalk. The players draw a 6-inch circle, and then draw a starting line about 6 feet away. At the starting line, each player tosses four coins, one at a time, toward the circle. The player whose coin lands the closest to the center of the circle is the winner, and he wins the rest of the coins. This player now takes one step closer to the circle. He tosses all coins at once toward the circle. He keeps the ones that land inside the circle. The coins that fall outside the circle go to the next player, who takes one step forward and tosses all of his coins. The process continues for the remaining players. At each turn, a player gets to take another step closer to the circle. Even when all players are standing around the circle, the game continues — until one player has won all the coins.

79 Frisbee Bowling

Best for Ages: 7 and up

Number of Players Required: 2 to 10

Equipment Needed: A frisbee, a driveway or sidewalk, and 10 cardboard tubes filled with clay, sand or dirt (if sand or dirt is used, the tubes should be taped shut).

How to Play: The players mark off a bowling lane and set up the tubes just like bowling pins. The game proceeds just like bowling, but with the frisbee as a bowling ball. Any frisbee toss that lands outside the lanes is a gutter ball.

80 Ghosts in the Graveyard

Best for Ages: 5 and up

Number of Players Required: 3 or more

Equipment Needed: None

How to Play: One player is chosen as the Ghost. The rest get in a circle and lie down. They're in the "graveyard," and they lie as still as possible. Meanwhile, the Ghost tries to make them move — without touching them in any way. The Ghost can make noises. She can yell, she can scream, she can laugh... or she can tell a joke. Anyone who moves or laughs becomes a ghost. The last player left is the winner and gets to be the Ghost for the next round.

81 Hopscotch

Best for Ages: 5 and up

Number of Players Required: 2 to 4

Equipment Needed: Chalk and a "potsy" or marker — something small and easy to toss, such as a stone, a coin or a bottlecap

How to Play: The game requires a flat playing surface, such as a driveway, sidewalk or dirt. First, the players diagram the playing area (see illustration). The side of each square should be about 18 inches to 2 feet long. The first player lines up at the start and tosses his potsy onto the first square. The player then hops onto the home square, landing on one foot. Next, skipping the first square, the player hops onto the second square. Then he hops onto each of the squares in the diagram. At squares 2-3, 5-6 and 8-9, he lands with one foot on each square. When he reaches the goal, the player hops around on one foot and then hops back through the squares. At square 2, he reaches down and picks up the potsy in

square 1 and then hops into home. As long as he's made no mistakes, the first player's turn continues. Now he tosses the potsy onto square 2, and hops through the squares again (this time avoiding square 2, both going out and coming back). Any of the following mistakes will end a player's turn:

★ stepping on a line.

★ missing the target square when tossing the potsy.

★ the potsy landing on a line.

★ landing on a square with someone else's potsy in it.

★ landing with two feet in a single square.

Any time a player makes a mistake, he leaves his marker in the last square it occupied and can't go again until it's his turn. Then the player repeats the last round before he can toss his potsy again. The first player to move his marker completely around the diagram to the goal and back to home is the winner.

Variations:

If enough squares are blocked by markers, players can draw "boxies" — temporary squares — next to the occupied squares and hop into them. Another variation is for players, on the way back to home, to kick the potsy into the next square. Still another variation calls for the players to balance the potsy on their head, a foot, or a finger while hopping back on the return to home. Hopscotch is sometimes called Potsy.

82 Hunt the Thimble

Best for Ages: 3 and up
Number of Players Required: 3 or more
Equipment Needed: A small object
How to Play: Hunt the Thimble is really a game of Hide and Seek, but it's a small object that's hidden and has to be found, not a player. One player, chosen as It, takes a small object (a thimble, coin, button or bottlecap will do) and places it where it can be seen — but not too easily. The rest of the players try to find it. The first player to find the object is the winner and gets to hide the object for the next round.

Variations:

In smaller playing areas, participants look for the object one-at-a-time. As the player gets close to the object, It says "Warm," "Getting Warmer," "Hot," or "Burning Hot." If the player starts to move away from the hidden object, It says "Cooling Off," "Cold" or "Ice Cold." In this version, the person who finds the object in the shortest amount of time is the winner.

In another version, each person who finds the object says nothing, but sits down — without revealing, in any way, the location of the object. The game is over when the last person finds the object. Players who have found the object can help guide the others by saying "Warm," "Cold," etc., along with It.

83 Jacks

Best for Ages: 7 and up

Number of Players Required: 2 or more

Equipment Needed: A small rubber ball and a half-dozen jacks (six-pointed objects that are available at many stores)

How to Play: First, a player tosses the jacks onto a flat surface such as a sidewalk or driveway. With one hand, the player tosses the ball up in the air. After it bounces, the player swipes one jack, then catches the ball (this is called "onesies"). The player tries to pick up two jacks on the next attempt ("twosies"), three after that (threesies), etc. The first player to successfully complete the pattern is the winner.

84 Jump Rope

Best for Ages: 5 and up

Number of Players Required: 3 or more

Equipment Needed: A jump rope

How to Play: Rope-skipping, which probably dates back to the discovery of hemp, is an activity that many children enjoy. Two players swing a rope, around 8 to 12 feet long — while one or two players hop over the rope at each turn. The players holding the rope swing slowly at first, then faster. The beat is maintained to rhymes like the following: *Mother, Mother, I am sick! Call for the doctor! Quick, quick, quick! In came the doctor, in came the nurse, in came the lady with the alligator purse! Out went the doctor, out went the nurse, out went the lady with the alligator purse! I went upstairs to make my bed, I made a mistake and I bumped my head! I went downstairs to milk the cow, I made a mistake and milked a sow! I went in the kitchen to bake a pie, I made a mistake and baked a fly!*

When the player misses a skip, she trades places with one of the others. Players keep count of the number of successful skips. Players can skip either on one foot, or both feet together.

Variation 1:

The same rules apply, but before the skipping begins, the players holding the rope chant: *Candy, candy, in the dish. How many pieces do you wish? One, two, three, four...etc.*

Brent and Becky, sitting in a tree, K-I-S-S-I-N-G! First comes love, then comes marriage, Then comes Becky with a baby carriage. How many babies did she have? One, two, three, four...etc.

Cinderella, dressed in yella, went outside to kiss her fella. By mistake, she kissed a snake, came back in with a belly-ache. How many doctors did it take? One, two, three, four... etc.

My little sister, dressed in pink, washed all the dishes in the kitchen sink. How many dishes did she break? One, two, three, four...etc.

The player begins to skip on the count of one. The players holding the rope keep count and change places on a miss. The player with the most successful jumps is the winner.

Variation 2:

For single jump-rope, the player swings the rope herself and skips, accompanied by the rhymes. Older players can try to swing the rope around twice on one jump. Playing tip: Players can end the game by jumping out of the skipping area or missing on purpose — often accompanied by rhymes like the following: *Jump rope, jump rope, when will I miss? Jump rope, jump rope, just watch this!*

I know a woman, her name is Miss. And all of a sudden, she goes like this!

85 Limbo

Best for Ages: 7 and up

Number of Players Required: 6 to 7

Equipment Needed: A broomstick or mop handle, called the limbo bar

How to Play: Lining up at opposite ends of the limbo bar, two players hold each end in the palms of their hands, at about chest level. One by one, the rest of the players try to get underneath the limbo bar without (a) bending forward or (b) touching the ground with their hands or knees. A player who knocks over the bar or touches the ground with anything but his feet is eliminated. After all players have passed under the bar, the bar is lowered to waist level and the players pass under again. The bar keeps going lower and lower until one player is left, and that player is the limbo champ.

Playing tip:

★   In the 1960s, a lively tune by rock-n-roll singer Chubby Checker called "Limbo Rock" was a big hit. Limbo is a lot more fun when the players whistle the tune and clap hands as each person passes under the bar.

86 O'Leary

Best for Ages: 7 and up

Number of Players Required: 3 or more

Equipment Needed: A bouncy ball

How to Play: O'Leary is a bouncing-ball game, in which the players chant a rhyme while bouncing the ball. On the fourth, eighth and 12th bounce, the player passes a leg over the ball, and on the 14th bounce, the player catches the ball. The rhyme goes like this: *One, two, three, O'Leary. Four, five, six, O'Leary. Seven, eight, nine, O'Leary. Ten, O'Leary. Catch me!* On each number, the player bounces the ball. On "O'Leary," the player passes a leg over the ball as it bounces. The player catches the ball as she says "Catch Me!" Anyone who fails to catch the ball or otherwise breaks the rhythm is out, and the last player left is the winner.

87 Pass the Ball

Best for Ages: 5 and up

Number of Players Required: 10 or more

Equipment Needed: Balls, apples or oranges

How to Play: This game is also called "Pass the Orange" or "Pass the Apple" (depending on what object the participants use to play). Players choose sides and line up. The first person in each group tucks a ball (or an orange or apple) under his chin. At the command "Go," the players try to pass the ball to the person next to him without using their hands. The player receiving the ball must also receive the ball under his chin. If the ball drops, the first person in line has to pick it up and start over again. The first team to get the ball to the end of the line is the winner.

88 Pin the Tail on the Donkey

Best for Ages: 5 and up

Number of Players Required: 3 or more

Equipment Needed: A blindfold, a drawing of a donkey with no tail and a donkey "tail" for each participant

How to Play: This party game is for children of all ages, and any number can play. The players need an outline of a donkey with no tail. The drawing can be on paper or cardboard and placed against a flat surface. Each player receives a donkey's "tail," made out of paper or cardboard. At the top of each tail is a piece of tape. One by one, each player is blindfolded and brought to a starting point about 10 feet from the donkey. The player is then turned around quickly three times. The player then tries to pin the tail on the donkey. Wherever he places the tail, the area is marked with his initials and the tail is removed. Then it's the next player's turn. The player who pins the tail closest to the right spot is the winner.

89 Scissors, Rock, Paper

Best for Ages: 5 and up

Number of Players Required: 2 or more

Equipment Needed: None

How to Play: Scissors, Rock, Paper requires each player to close his hand into a fist, then shape it into one of three shapes: Scissors (index and middle finger extended), Rock (closed fist) or Paper (flat hand, facing downward). Two players square off. Together, with one fist closed, they say "One strikes three, Shoot!" and then quickly thrust their fists forward, making either the scissors, rock or paper shape. Here's how the winner is decided:

★ If the players have the same shape, it's a tie and they go again.

★ When its scissors versus paper, scissors win, since scissors cut paper.

★ When it's stone versus scissors, stone wins, since stones can break scissors

★ When it's paper versus stone, paper wins, since paper covers stone.

Best two-of-three is the winner, and winners move on to the next round until one player is left.

90 Whirligig

Best for Ages: 9 and up

Number of Players Required: 5 to 10

Equipment Needed: A 12-foot rope and an old sneaker

How to Play: After a turn as It in Whirligig, a player will gladly give it up to someone else. The players get a 12-foot rope and tie an object at one end, such as an old sneaker. One player is chosen as It and holds the rope at the other end. It begins swinging the rope in a circle. The other players have to jump over the rope as it comes toward them. The player in the middle can raise the rope, lower it, make it go faster or slow it down. Any player touched by the rope is eliminated. So is any player who falls. Players take turns spinning the rope, since nobody can be It for too long in this game.

PART 5:

Word and Mind Games

91 Alphabet Travels

Best for Ages: 10 and up
Number of Players Required: 3 or more
Equipment Needed: None
How to Play: Each player must make up a sentence in which the nouns, verbs and adjectives begin with the same letter. The players go in alphabetical order. For example: First player: "I'm going to Alabama to ask for an ancient aunt." Second player: "I'm going to Brazil to bake beautiful bananas." Third player: "I'm going to Canada to catch some cranky cougars." Fourth player: "I'm going to Detroit to deliver a dizzy dinosaur." Fifth player: "I'm going to England to escape from an evil electrician." Any player who can't construct a sentence with the right letters during a set time period is out of the game. The last player left in the game is the winner.

92 Bodies

Best for Ages: 5 and up

Number of Players Required: 2 or more

Equipment Needed: None

How to Play: One player is chosen as the Leader. The leader stands in front of the other players and points to a body part, saying "Eye, eye, eye," or "Nose, nose, nose." The other players must then point to the body part that the Leader names. At some point, the Leader touches one body part, but names another. For example, she points to her ear and says "Arm, arm arm." Anyone who points to the wrong body part — that is, the body part that the Leader points to, but didn't name, is out. The last player left gets to be the leader for the next game. This game is sometimes called "Pavlov's Dogs."

93 Buzz

Best for Ages: 7 and up
Number of Players Required: 2 or more
Equipment Needed: None
How to Play: One player starts to count, saying "One!" The next player sounds off with "Two," and the counting continues until it's time for a number that's divisible by seven or has a seven in it. Moving at a quick pace, the counting should go like this: "One." "Two." "Three." "Four." "Five." "Six." "Buzz!" The next buzz number would be 14, followed by 17, 21, 27, 28, 35, 37, etc. A player who says a number when she should have said "buzz" is out of the game. The count continues with that same number. The last player left wins.

Variation:

Players can use any one-digit number besides 7.

94 Camel

Best for Ages: 5 and up

Number of Players Required: 3 or more

Equipment Needed: None

How to Play: One player, the Guesser, leaves the group, which then comes up with a secret word that the Guesser must discover. One at a time, each player must make up a sentence using that word — preferably a word with several homonyms. Players must, however, substitute the word "camel" for the secret word. For example, if the secret word is "sun," the game would go something like this:

First player: "When the camel comes out, the birds start singing."

Second player: "I'm my father's only camel."

Third player: "Those clouds are blocking the camel."

When the Guesser correctly identifies the secret word, she changes places with the last player to make a sentence.

95 "Crambo," the Rhyming Mystery Word Game

Best for Ages: 10 and up

Number of Players Required: 3 or more

Equipment Needed: None

How to Play: All but forgotten today, this was one of the most popular word games of the 19th century. One player is chosen as the Guesser, and moves out of hearing range of the rest of the players, who select a word. When the Guesser comes back, she is given one word that rhymes with the secret word. The Guesser must then try to figure out other words that rhyme with the secret word, but without saying them. For example, let's say the secret word is "noon," and the hint given to the Guesser is "June." The questioning would go like this:

  Guesser: "Is it something you use when you eat?"

  Players: "No, it isn't a spoon."

  Guesser: "Is it something you sing?"

  Players: "No, it's not a tune."

The questions continue until the Guesser comes up with the right idea. If the Guesser says something like, "Is it when we go to lunch?" then the other players know she knows the right answer and that round is over.

96 Geography

Best for Ages: 10 and up

Number of Players Required: 2 or more

Equipment Needed: None

How to Play: One player is chosen to go first. She names a city, state or country. The next player must name another from the same category. Whichever he says, however, has to begin with the same letter as the last letter of the city, state or country named by the first player. For example:

First player: "Miami!"

Second Player: "Indianapolis!"

Third Player: "St. Louis!"

Fourth Player: "St. Paul!"

Fifth Player: "Louisville!"

Any player who is unable to name a city, state or country with the appropriate letter is out. The last player left is the winner.

Variation:

Younger players can take part in a similar game, but by substituting first names, animals or colors for cities, states and countries.

97 Laugh Contest

Best for Ages: 5 and up
Number of Players Required: 2 or more
Equipment Needed: None
How to Play: The object of this game is not to laugh. Any even number can take part. Players match up and stare at each other, making faces, telling jokes, making weird sounds and doing anything else to make an opponent laugh. The first player to laugh is out, and the winner moves on to face another opponent. The last player left is the winner.

Playing tip:

★ Physical contact is strictly against the rules, but players can get as close to an opponent as possible, as long as they don't make contact.

98 Riddley Riddley Ree

Best for Ages: 5 and up

Number of Players Required: 2 or more

Equipment Needed: None

How to Play: "Riddley Riddley Ree, I see something you don't see!" is the mantra that begins this game, which provides a breather from the rigors of physical activity.

One player is designated as the Riddler. The Riddler selects a stationary object that's in plain view of all players. The Riddler gives only one clue at the start of the game — the color of the object she sees. Each player can ask a set number of questions — one at a time — about what the Riddler sees. The Riddler is required to give only "yes" or "no" answers. A player can't ask, for example, "How big is it?" Instead, to get an idea of size, a player must ask questions like, "Is it bigger than a car?" or "Can it fit through a door?"

Players are allowed a set number of questions, depending on the number and age of the participants. At any time, a player can try to guess the object the Riddler sees. An incorrect guess, however, means that player can't take any more turns. Here's an example, with the Riddler looking at a backyard birdbath:

Riddler: Riddley, riddley, ree, I see something you don't see — and it's gray!

Player #1: Is it alive?

Riddler: No.

Player #2: Is it made of wood?

Riddler: No.

Player #3: Is it on the ground?

Riddler: Yes.

Player #4: Is it smaller than a door?

Riddler: Yes.

Player #5: Is it dark gray?

Riddler: Yes.

Player #1: Is it that watering can near the hose?

Riddler: No. You're out!

Player #2: Is it made of stone?

Riddler: Yes.

Player #3: Does it stay in the same place all the time?

Riddler: Yes.

Player #4: Does it have any parts that move?

Riddler: No.

Player #5: Is it that birdbath in the neighbors' yard?

Riddler: Yes! Your turn to be the Riddler!

If the Riddler stumps the other players, she takes another turn. A player who makes the right guess gets a chance to be the Riddler.

99 Staring Contest

Best for Ages: 3 and up

Number of Players Required: 2 or more

Equipment Needed: None

How to Play: This game is very popular with little ones. Participants match up, and each pair stares at each other as long as possible without blinking. The first player to blink is out, and the winner moves on to the next round. The last player left is the winner.

Playing tip:

★ This is not to be confused with the Laugh Contest, where anything goes. The best bet is to keep a straight face!

100 Telephone

Best for Ages: 5 and up
Number of Players Required: 4 or more
Equipment Needed: None
How to Play: Known as Whispers in the United Kingdom, this game can involve any number of players age 5 or older. One player is chosen by lot to begin the game, while all other players gather in a circle. The first player whispers a one-sentence "secret" to the player on her left (players must listen carefully, because the secret can only be told once). That player, in turn, tells the secret to the next player. When the last player hears the secret, he repeats it out loud. Then the player who started the game tells the original secret. With enough players, the secret usually gets completely scrambled from start to finish.

101 Twenty Questions

Best for Ages: 9 and up
Number of Players Required: 2 or more
Equipment Needed: None
How to Play: Here's another game that gives everyone a chance to catch their breath or relax in the shade on a hot day. Twenty Questions is similar to Riddley Riddley Ree, but the person asking the questions — the Riddler — doesn't have to choose objects that are visible. The Riddler can select an animal, a person, a TV show, or just about anything else. Let's say the Riddler is thinking about George Washington. He starts the game with: "I'm thinking of a famous person." Then the players can start asking questions that require yes/no or either/or answers. They can ask no more than 20.

Player #1: Is this person alive or dead?

Riddler: Dead.

Player #2: Was this person a man or a woman?

Riddler: A man.

Player #3: Was he an American?

Riddler: Yes.

Player #4: Was he a sports star?

Riddler: No.

Player #1: Was he an actor?

Riddler: No.

Player #2: Was he in government?

Riddler: Yes.

Player #3: Was he a president?

Riddler: Yes

Player #4: Is it Lincoln?

Riddler: No! You're out!

After the players ask a combined total of twenty questions and they still don't have an answer, each player can make one guess. Anyone who guesses correctly becomes the Riddler. If the Riddler stumps the other players, he gets another turn.

Bibliography & Indexes

BIBLIOGRAPHY

Arnold, Arnold. *The World Book of Children's Games*. New York: World Publishing, 1972.

Beaver, Patrick. *Victorian Parlor Games*. Nashville: Thomas Nelson Inc., 1974.

Cole, Joanna , and Stephanie Calmenson. *Rain or Shine Activity Book*. New York: Morrow Junior Books, 1997.

Crisfield, D.W. *Pick-Up Games: The Rules, The Players, The Equipment*. New York: Facts On File, 1993.

Foster, Sally. *Simon Says . . . Let's Play*. New York: Cobblehill Books, 1990.

Gryski, Camilla. *Let's Play: Traditional Games of Childhood*. Buffalo: Kids Can Press Ltd., 1998.

Hall, Godfrey. *Traditions Around the World: Games*. New York: Thomson Learing, 1995.

Langstaff, John, and Carol Langstaff. *Shimmy Shimmy Coke-Ca-Pop!* Garden City: Doubleday & Company, Inc., 1973.

Seymour, Harold. *Baseball: The Early Years*. New York: Oxford University Press, 1960.

Sierra, Judy, and Robert Kaminski. *Children's Traditional Games*. Phoenix: The Oryx Press, 1984.

Vecchione, Glen. *The World's Best Street and Yard Games*. New York: Sterling Publishing Co., 1989.

— *The World's Best Outdoor Games*. New York: Sterling Publishing Co., 1992.

Wallechinsky, David. *The Complete Book of the Summer Olympics* (1996 edition). Boston: Little, Brown and Company, 1996.

INDEXES

About the Author

A native of Staten Island, N.Y., Pete Cava's involvement in sports and media dates back to his youth. Cava played high school football, CYO basketball and youth league baseball, and also wrote for his school newspaper and took part in a student-run radio station in Brooklyn. At Fordham University he was a statistician for the baseball team and organized a Staten Island sandlot club. While serving with the First Infantry Division at Fort Riley, KS, he wrote for the post newspaper.

Cava joined the national staff of USA Track & Field (USATF), then known as The Athletics Congress, when it began operations in 1979. He headed press operations at many national championships in the United States, including the 1984 World Cross Country Championships in East Rutherford, N.J., and the inaugural World Indoor Track and Field Championships in Indianapolis in 1987. He also served as a United States team press officer for international track competitions in Europe, Asia and Australia, and worked as a network television researcher at the Olympic Games in Los Angeles, Seoul and Barcelona. Cava is a life member of the International Society of Olympic Historians and belongs to the Association of Track and Field Statisticians and the Federation of American Statisticians of Track. He also serves on the Board of Directors of the National Track and Field Hall of Fame.

After leaving USATF in 1998, Cava formed International Sports Associates, a writing/research/public relations firm. In 1999 he was a media consultant for the NCAA Indoor Track and Field Championships and served as a United States Olympic Committee press officer at the World University Games in Palma de Mallorca, Spain, and the Pan American Games in Winnipeg, Canada. Other ISA clients include American Sports Nutrition and Indiana Olympians.

Mom's Handy Book of Backyard Games is Cava's second published book. He is also the author of *Tales from the Cubs Dugout* (Sports Publishing, 1999) and he is hard at work on *The Encyclopedia of Indiana-Born Major League Baseball Players*. His articles on Hoosier big leaguers have appeared in *Baseball Digest, Sports Collectors Digest, The New York Times, The Indianapolis Star* and over a dozen other newspapers throughout the country. He is also the author of scholarly histories of the New York Mets and Olympic baseball, as well as a scholarly treatise on re-porter-turned-short-story-writer Ring Lardner. A member of the Society for American Baseball Research, he is also a part-time member of *The Indianapolis Star*'s sports department and serves as an official scorer for the Indianapolis Indians.